FAMOUS BIBLE PEOPLE
CHILDREN
WITH FOLD·OUT PAGES

Written by Daryl Lucas
Illustrated by Robert C. Durham

Tyndale House Publishers, Inc.
Wheaton, Illinois

ISAAC

"Dad, where is the lamb?" Isaac asked. "We have wood. We have flint to start the fire. But we don't have a lamb to sacrifice."

"God will provide a lamb," said Abraham. "He will provide it when we get there."

"OK," said Isaac. Isaac and his father had sacrificed to God many times. They always did it the same way. First they made a table of stones. Then they put firewood on the table. Finally, they killed a lamb and burned it.

Isaac put down his armful of wood. But he didn't see any lamb. Abraham put the wood on the table of stones. Then he tied up Isaac's feet. He placed his son on the firewood.

Isaac did not speak. He knew his dad would never want to hurt him. He trusted God too. But he felt scared. Where was the lamb? Would God really provide?

SAMUEL

Samuel awoke with a start.
Someone had called his name in
the night. He got up and ran to
his guardian, Eli. "Here I am, sir.
You called me."

Eli awoke and looked sleepily
at Samuel. "I did not call you,"
Eli whispered. "Go back to
bed." Samuel went back to bed,
wondering whom he had heard.

"Samuel!" someone said
again. Samuel got up again and
went to Eli. "Yes?" said Samuel.
"You called me."

"I didn't call you," said Eli. "Go back to sleep." Samuel went back to bed, puzzled. Who was calling him? The voice was real. It wasn't a dream. But there was no one else in the temple. If it wasn't Eli, who was it?

Samuel pulled the covers to his chin. He couldn't sleep. Would the voice call him again?

DAVID

Nine-foot-tall Goliath started toward the boy David. As Goliath walked, the ground shook. His 200-pound armor clanked.

David kicked at the dirt. "You think you're great," he yelled out. "But your sword and spear are useless. God is on my side!"

The soldiers in Goliath's army laughed. "You little pest!" Goliath sneered. "Your stick and your sling are useless! Fight me, and you'll be sorry!"

David had no weapons and no armor. He had only a shepherd's staff and a sling. But Goliath was a champion fighter. His sword weighed twenty-five pounds. Goliath came closer and closer to David.

The soldiers on David's side were afraid. What could David do against a mighty soldier? How could he possibly win?

JOASH

Jehoiada the priest greeted Prince Joash. "Come on," said Jehoiada. "Now's the time!" He grabbed the prince by the hand, and off they went.

Seven-year-old Joash was nervous. Wicked Queen Athaliah hated him. She wanted him dead. That's why he had been hiding for six years.

Jehoiada led Joash to the temple courtyard. The prince felt shivers at what he saw. The courtyard was filled with people. Many rulers were there. Many

priests and Levites were there. Army officers were there. "Wow," Joash whispered.

Several men rushed up to Joash. They had swords in their hands. Other men with swords stood at the gate. Nobody could get in or out.

Just then, everyone became quiet. They looked at Joash. The soldiers drew their swords. What was going to happen next?

JAIRUS'S DAUGHTER

Jairus's little twelve-year-old girl was very sick. She needed help right away. But none of the doctors could do anything. She was dying.

Jairus heard that Jesus could heal people. So he went to see Jesus. He begged Jesus to heal his little daughter.

"Oh yes," said Jesus, "I will heal her." Jesus began to go with him back to his home. But before they got there, messengers stopped them.

"It's too late, Jairus," they said. "Your daughter is already dead."

Jairus and his wife cried and cried.

"Do not be sad," said Jesus. "Everything will be all right. Just trust in me."

But Jairus and his wife kept crying. They loved their little daughter. Now she was dead. What could Jesus do for her now?

THE BOY WHO SHARED HIS LUNCH

It was getting late. The crowd of 5,000 families was far away from home. Everyone was hungry, and no one had any food. No one, that is, but one small boy.

A man named Andrew walked up to the boy. "Jesus wants to feed the crowd," he said. "Does your family have any food?"

"I have five rolls and two fishes," said the boy.

"You are the only one in the whole crowd with food," said Andrew. Andrew brought the boy

to Jesus. The little boy gave his food to Jesus. He did not know what else to do. His food surely wouldn't feed 5,000 families.

"Have everyone sit down," Jesus told Andrew. The little boy sat down with the crowd. Why did Jesus take his food? It wasn't enough to feed the crowd. Was Jesus going to eat it all himself? Was he going to give it to his friends?

Read more about these
CHILDREN
in the Bible

ISAAC

In the Old Testament

Genesis 22:5-14

SAMUEL

In the Old Testament

1 Samuel 3:2-14

DAVID

In the Old Testament

1 Samuel 17:32-51

JOASH

In the Old Testament

2 Chronicles 23:1-11

JAIRUS'S DAUGHTER

In the New Testament

Mark 5:21-24, 35-43

THE BOY WHO SHARED HIS LUNCH

In the New Testament

John 6:2-13